Sacred Breath
Understanding the electrical power source of the human body and how to keep it charged.

D'Lana O'Neal

All rights reserved. No part of this book may be reproduced in any form or by any electronic or mechanical means, including information storage and retrieval systems, without the permission of the author. Exceptions will be allowed by reviewers for the purpose of quoting brief excerpts.

All scriptures, unless otherwise noted, are taken from the New International Version of the Holy Bible.

Editorial Contribution and Book Design:
D'LANA O'NEAL/Unshackled Ministries

Cover Graphics & Design:

Printed in the United States of America
Library of Congress Literary Work

Copyright © 2024 by D' Lana O'Neal

ISBN: 979-8-9899590-20

CONTENTS

Acknowledgments	v
Dedication	vii
Forward	ix
Introduction: The Sacred Breath	xi
Chapter 1: The sacred breath is the power of God	1
Chapter 2: The sacred breath gives and restores life	4
Chapter 3: The sacred breath is our daily substance	11
Chapter 4: The sacred breath is our counselor	16
Chapter 5: The sacred breath is our vital force	21

ACKNOWLEDGEMENTS

This book could not have been written without the many people God placed in my life when I needed them most. Dr. Robin Mitchell, thank you for listening to the voice of God when he told you to put all your seed in the ground, that I might have life again and have it to the full.

When it came to addressing my health concerns, in faith you stood tall against all odds, looking into the face of a bleak situation with surmounting courage. When others gave up, you went all in, and I will forever be grateful to you for that.

Because of your faith, not only did my health and life begin to transform; you built the faith of your team as they worked alongside you.

People all over the world will know you because you have become part of my story, the story I now get to tell. You allowed your faith in what God could do through you fuel your passion to help me and others who would come after me. That same faith that launched my healing process has also inspired me to become an advocate for natural health. Thank you!

Dr. Asar Hapi, after receiving all the nutrients my body was deficient in and later hitting a plateau in my healing process, I felt hopeless and sought God for more answers and a better understanding. In your humility you invited me to sit at your feet and learn the secrets of the vital force. I will forever cherish those lessons and the stories that helped bring them to life. I will use them as my foundational tools for teaching others as they are becoming more deeply rooted in my daily practice.

I thank God for his undeniable wisdom and giving you the eyes of an eagle to see the need and pour into me. I especially thank you for unveiling to me the power of this sacred breath, its vital force and connection to God. Now that I'm aware of its role in my life, I'm committed to protecting and utilizing its functions with intentionality as I embrace the power that accompanies it. May God continue to use you as a great vessel, blessing the work of your hands.

To my spiritual family, you are my greatest supporters and my biggest group of fans. My heart beats stronger because of you. Thank you for your countless prayers, endless nights of serving me, and your patience as we all waited for the outcomes on my natural path.

I am so grateful that you continued the course with me, never failing to give wholeheartedly. I know it must have been very difficult after not seeing many results, but you allowed my faith and desire to do it naturally to be enough for you to keep giving your support.

The air we breathe is sacred and as I take each breath, I'm reminded of the life I now get to enjoy with each of you. When I laugh, I'm able to do so with a richer and heartier chuckle, remembering the days when it was as faint as a whisper. Let's enjoy this sacred breath!

To my many friends, thank you for sharing this journey with me. I can't think of a time when you were needed and were not there. Thank you for the many prayers that you sent out for me.

DEDICATION

I dedicate this body of work to anyone who has ever experienced the feelings of fatigue and the mechanical breakdown of the human body due to aging. Those who spent hundreds of dollars trying to recapture a small fraction of the energy they possessed while in the prime of their youth. You are not alone; regaining this energy and restoring your normal function is now possible. However, you won't get those results from visiting your local gym or a bottled energy drink. This energy source is powered by life's inescapable partner, The Sacred Breath.

As you read this book, may you be enlightened to look at your breath, body, and quality of your life in an entirely new way. You will now have access to the power to change not only your level of energy, but so much more!

FORWARD

This book is a must read for everyone who wants to understand the relationship between God and the power that He gives each of us to heal and be well. D'Lana did an excellent job of taking the Bible, her health study, and correlating the temple of God with the human body and how we are to care for it. Her biblical understanding of the secrecy, holiness, and care of the temple of God is not only captured, but it also serves as a model for others to understand our bodily temple in which God lives by His Holy Spirit.

The Sacred Breath shares the mystery of the healing process, a variety of health elements, and the knowledge of science and proper nutrition, and how it all connects.

As a witness to her healing journey, I applaud her tenacity for life and passion to share this important work with others. D'Lana's commitment to her own health and wellness catapulted her to the head of my class in which I granted her an invitation to learn the secrets of the breath. Her approach to mastering the concepts of health and wellness by addressing the whole person—mind, body, and spirit—was key to the restoration of her vitality. With this breath work as her primary tool, this unique approach now lays a broader foundation for the practitioners who come into the field after her.

The Sacred Breath is an invitation to look at our body and the healing of it in new ways. It places each person in the driver's seat, directing their own level of wellness and its destination. If we want to experience the fullness that life offers us, we now have that opportunity being granted through our awareness of the Sacred Breath.

The Sacred Breath is a powerful tool and equips all who dare to practice it with a new message, "I shall live life to the full and not die!"

Dr. Asar Hapi

Dr. Asar Hapi creator of the ANCAR 2000 breath system. He holds three PhDs as a Physician of Naturopath, a Chiropractor, and an Acupuncturist. He is also a grandmaster in the yogic science of kinetic yoga and a Physician of Oriental medicine.

INTRODUCTION
The Sacred Breath

Our life and what we do with our breath is a constant balancing act. I say "act" because when we begin to understand the significance of the sacred breath and our responsibility that comes with that gift, it will call us all to action.

We must begin to look at breathing with a new set of lenses. This new outlook will help us to cultivate a greater understanding and appreciation for the gift the sacred breath is to humanity.

When we are born into the world, for the most part we come out mute, without the ability to make a sound. Our noses and mouths are suctioned out and we are given a whack on our bottom. If we are chosen to receive the gift of life, God blows his deposit of the sacred breath into us and we belt out a holy cry. This is not only an acknowledgement of this precious gift of life; it serves as our first encounter with God himself. It is through this deposit that we will now share a part of him.

When one passes through the birth canal, if God doesn't gift life, no amount of oxygen will suffice. God is the Creator and only He can give life through this sacred breath.

Although this experience of receiving breath is monumental, the excitement of the first breath fades as the days go by. Unless there is a problem with this process, most will go on their way breathing their entire life's span without a second thought.

The sacred breath goes unnoticed by most, until faced with a life altering breath restricting illness (asthma, bronchitis, COPD, upper respiratory infections, and the like), or a near death experience that causes one to stop and take notice.

Like most near death experiences, some walk away never the same again, as they are fully aware of their near-death escape and near loss of the scared breath. Others are unaware of the message behind the experience and continue their previous path in life without much change.

I was impacted by a near death experience that changed my life as I once knew it. In May 2014, I was told as a result of my declining health, my organs had begun shutting down and I was given a very short span of time before they shut down completely, and life as I knew it would end. After many years of experiencing symptoms that resulted in inconclusive test results, I decided to take an alternative approach to restorative health. I set out to find and commit myself to a holistic treatment plan. If the results panned out, my plan was to become an advocate to help others looking for alternative restorative health options.

During this time, I felt as if I had experienced a good life compared to some, but I had not left my footprint and wanted to do so. Fueled by passion, I began my search for natural alternatives. On my journey to discover better alternatives and purpose, I was introduced to the ANCAR 2000 breath system Dr. Hapi created. I call it the "sacred breath."

The uncovering of the sacred breath has given me the motivation to go in search of what the "life to the full" that God promised looks like. What was it that the enemy tried to take from me through premature death? Through my search for understanding, I now have an awareness of this sacred breath (ANCAR 2000 System) and how it fuels the body's energy and operating systems. This wellness experience provides an opportunity to experience life to the full to those who practice it. I now get the privilege to share this life changing experience with others.

In his early twenties, Dr. Asar Hapi had his own near-death experience that laid the foundation for the birthing of the ANCAR 2000 breath system in 1994.

He now holds three PhDs as a Physician of Naturopath, a Chiropractor, and an Acupuncturist. He is a grandmaster in the yogic science of kinetic yoga and a Physician of Oriental medicine. He is one of the few that performs a system called needleless acupuncture. Dr. Hapi has spent a considerable amount of time creating and perfecting the sacred breath naturopathic modality, which I was a recipient of and now am a student of this healing practice.

The ANCAR 2000 is a dynamic holistic health care program, which utilizes fire breathing techniques to enhance and increase the development of the body's systems, promoting optimal levels of wellness. ANCAR 2000 stands for athletic, neuro, cardio, aerobic regeneration. This technique concentrates on the nervous system and its regenerative abilities to improve the body wellness and function, without the physical exertion from a workout. It is based on physical strengthening that occurs inside of body while transforming the outside.

The ANCAR 2000 differs from other care because it focuses on Naturopathic Modalities such as energy flow. Through a variety of patterns, speeds, and practice, an increase of energy will flow to the different muscles and body systems. Using the breathing system alone can strengthen the Prana Vital Force and improve cellular function and energy levels to muscles and ligaments.

The origin of Naturopath Medicine
Naturopathic medicine (or naturopathy) is an alternative medical practice based on the belief that the body can heal itself. Dr. Benedict Lust, MD is credited for bringing naturopathy to America and forming the profession after being cured by Father Kneipp and studying under many prominent naturopaths in Europe.

The origin of yogic science of Kinetic Yoga
The practice of Kinetic Yoga is over 5000 years ago. The history of this practice is recorded in a book called *The Egyptian Book of the Dead's* (but it is really the Egyptian book of coming alive). Under the mastery of this Kinetic Yoga practice, one will learn the secrets of being light like a cat, containing both balance and flexibility, with the strength of a bull. Dr. Hapi's system helps to develop the power of each client's personal

electrical power source to their full capacity. The ancients call this yoga; yoga to calm the spirit being within. We are spirits living in our bodies of matter. The practice of this yoga system provides strength over matter (the body). Through breath work, the mind will have power and complete control over matter to keep it balanced.

Additional tools to help recharge the electrical power
The Creator created stones that carry powerful energy sources. Published research shares the impact that stones can have on the body's health and well-being. A crystal is a stone that embodies a powerful energy source and can charge up your chakras when worn on your body, particularly around your neck in the pathway of the chakras. There are seven major electric circuits called Chakras: Root, Sacral, Solar Plexus, Heart, Throat, Third Eye, and the Crown, and fourteen minors called meridians. The seven Chakras run through the center of the body where the energy source flows through them. These Chakras are energy sources in the body and vital to the healing process of the mind, body, and spirit. If the Chakras lose power, they can be recharged through a variety of natural modalities.

How does the sacred breath work?
How is this power created? The power is created through the two nostril gateways and is referred to as the generator. The generator generates power in the middle of the body; the ancients refer this area of the body as the solar plexus. Our gut area is the core of the body, where all energy sources and body movements flow. A whopping 70 percent of our immune system is in our digestive tract—our digestive tract is where a variety of bacteria live, both good and bad. This power source, or fire, kills and prevents microbial organisms from living in the comforts of our immune system or gut.

The ancients held this secret knowledge of the breath for centuries, sharing it with only a few that have gone through the fire of testing and found to be worthy recipients of the secrets to life. These individuals have inherited the responsibility to provide healing to others through its ancient modality and practice.

Although this use of energy practice is ancient, some believe the era of solar energy is a new-age movement. We see society now becoming more aware of its presence and the wide varieties of its usages. Recent research has used magnets and certain metals like copper to aid support with the body's normal functions.

While studies are still being conducted on this subject, many are currently capitalizing on the production of this electrical energy source. We see a wave of usages popping up all around us such as solar panels for homes, boats, power outages, and more. If you have ever seen the large windmills, mostly in farmland areas off the highways, they are producing massive amounts of reusable electrical power. In the same way, your nasal passages are generating high levels of electrical voltage to allow your body's class-nine systems to function. These eleven organ or systems include the integumentary system, skeletal system, muscular system, lymphatic system, respiratory system, digestive system, nervous system, endocrine system, cardiovascular system, urinary system, and reproductive systems. With precision, skill, and accuracy, the nose can generate a combustion of power in the middle of your core that gives your body the ability to operate all systems, including breaking down the food you eat, extracting the nutrients from the food, and processing out what remains through elimination. One of the most significant systems of the body is the digestive, largely because proper digestion is critical and impacts all the other systems.

You may recall the saying of a cat having nine lives. Let's note where the concept originated. The nine systems of the body are supposed to be kept alive with your breath. We are not breathing on our own, but we are being breathed. We were created without an awareness of this breath; totally depending on God for life through it. Have you ever heard someone say I CAN'T BREATHE?

The cat is a symbol and is used to reflect the ancient secrets and power over the nine systems of the body. It's more than a myth, but its symbolism and holds a powerful truth to the relationship of the body's strength, balance and flexibility capabilities. If you ever visit Kimmett in

Northern Africa, you will see a pharaoh face on the spitz. The pharaoh's hidden message says, "I have the secrets over these nine systems to my body. I have mastered the secrets of the power of the pyramid (the breath through the gateways of the nose) to keep these nine systems alive and functioning properly."

The body uses electrical energy to do everything, even to blink your eyes. If you use any touch screen electronic devices, with every touch of the screen, you are utilizing electrical energy from your body's power source. This system is called your nervous system, in which small electrical currents travel through your fingertips to activate the computer's touch command. This modern technology engages your electrical circuitry (nervous system) to operate the device.

If you take in large amounts of heavy foods into the body for nourishment but lack the amount of electrical power necessary to process it, your body's organs will become over exerted and will break down over time. In Naprapathy, we call it a blown or short circuit; the medical terminology refers to it as a stroke.

There is a book called *Back to Eden* by Jethro Kloss that teaches the types of food that require less combustible energy to process, how to maintain optimal health with proper nutrition, and which foods to eat to heal the body. The same is true with emotional, spiritual, and other physical processing. We are mind, body, and spirit; therefore, we need to address all three of these components in order to maintain or restore the body to optimal health.

The sacred breath modalities address the eleven systems of the body and with regular practice, proper nutrition, and rest, if your body hasn't been run into the ground, the body can be restored to its optimal condition.

The Sacred Breath will walk you through five descriptions of the breath, each filled with information that will make you stop to check your breath, change the way you think about breathing and hopefully motivate you to learn more.

CHAPTER 1: THE SACRED BREATH IS THE POWER OF GOD

From the beginning of existence, God's incredible power has been fully displayed. He has an uncontainable, unrestricted, and unleashing power in His breath. We can see the power of His breath when He speaks throughout the 1st chapter of Genesis. In these quotes below we witness power unfold behind the breath of God's spoken words.

In Genesis 1:3, God said, "Let there be light," and there was light. With His breath, God spoke light into a dark world.

In Genesis 1:6, God said, "Let there be expansion between the waters to separate water from water." With His breath alone He established the expansion in the water. This did not happen by any other way; this happened through the power of the breath of God alone.

In Genesis 1:9, God said, "Let the water under the sky be gathered to one place, and let dry ground appear." We see the universe being ushered in by the sacred breath of God.

In Genesis 1:11, God said, "Let the land produce vegetation: seed-bearing plants and trees on the land that bear fruit with seed in it, according to their various kinds." We see that God is not just putting things in place for the moment; He's intentionally planning by calling forth fruit bearing plants and trees.

In Genesis 1:14, God said, "Let there be lights in the expanse of the sky to separate day from night and let them serve as signs to mark seasons and days and years and let them be lights in the expanse of the sky to give light on the earth."

In Genesis 1:20, God said, "Let the water teem with living creatures, and let birds fly above the earth across the expanse of the sky." After God created these living creatures, he also breathed life into their bodies.

In Genesis 1:24, God said, "Let the land produce living creatures according to their kinds: livestock, creatures that move along the ground, and wild animals, each according to its kind."

In Genesis 1:26, there was a conversation that took place in heaven between God the Father, God the Son, and God the Holy Spirit. In Genesis 1:26 God said, "Let us [signifying the presence of the Trinity] create man in our image." In all that God created with His creative splendor, not one thing could survive without His sacred breath. (See also: Genesis 2:7)

To demonstrate the breath's power, let's compare the human body to a motor vehicle. The breath must be balanced as it relates to our movement. We can't drive on the expressway if our car can only go 10-15 miles per hour. Pushing the gas pedal to the floor in an effort to produce more power will be unproductive.

In a motor vehicle, the alternator is a generator of electrical power and is key to the charging capabilities. When an engine is running, the alternator charges the battery and supplies additional electrical power for the vehicle's other electrical systems. Without the battery having its necessary level of charging power to put the electrical components to work, the car won't move.

Our human body functions much like a car. The solar plexus in our body is our alternator and generator's powering system. When we are practicing breath work, we are generating electrical power through the wind turbine (intense breathing through the gateways of the nose). This power is then used to charge our batteries (heart, kidneys) and generate additional electrical power used for the lungs and other organs as needed.

Without understanding the power of the sacred breath, how to use, conserve, replenish, protect, and reboot it, we will undoubtedly run into many associated health problems without realizing. The power is in knowing the breath and the proper utilization of it for all functions of our body.

CHAPTER 2: THE SACRED BREATH GIVES AND RESTORES LIFE

The power of the sacred breath restores life to our bodies. If a baby isn't breathing when it is born, the doctor hits the baby on the tailbone to spark the kundalini (the internal energy force) that allows the baby to emit that first holler. In that holler, the baby activates the esoteric (internal electrical pump) power source to begin building the electrical charge. This superpower gives the body the ability to take in liquid milk, extracting the nutrients and discarding the waste as a solid. During the time they spend crying or screaming, the solar plexus creates a wind turbine that builds up an enormous electrical power charge and reserve. The baby didn't lift weights or run any laps around a track to build strength to turn over, crawl, sit up, or eventually pull itself up to stand and later walk. Where in the world did the baby get the physical energy and strength to do all these things? The baby didn't have a personal trainer; this surmounting power was built through the utilization of the sacred breath. Through crying, this mechanical movement (contracting and releasing the internal springs) was generating electrical power by the deep, rapid, inhalation and exhalation process.

When I got the news of my body being in an unfavorable condition, beyond repair, and denied access to a referral for nutritional support, I thought to myself, "If God can breathe life into dry bones, he can breathe new life into the parts of my dying organs."

In Ezekiel 37:1-14, the prophet Ezekiel prophesied about the restoration of his people Israel. In a prophetic vision, the Lord said he would make breath enter the dry bones and they would come to life. This is not just a nice story in the Bible; it is true and those who believe in the healing and restorative power of God get to eat its fruit. The prophet Ezekiel was no stranger to this healing power of God. This image of the sacred breath of God restoring life to a valley of dead, dry bones inspired me and gave me hope. With fervent prayers offered up to God for resources and miraculous healing, my search began for homeopathic doctors.

When we were created, we were formed with three components of power that our bodies need to operate at an optimal level. These power components are chemical, electrical, and mechanical. While the sacred breath provides and restores life, the things we do, think, feel, or experience impact the body's power components as well. These power components not only support our body functions; when balanced, they provide support to the eleven systems in our body and give them the ability to regulate themselves. When they are not balanced and other important nutritional support is lacking, we can become vulnerable to sickness and disease. With improper balances of these three components, the body's physical, mental, and emotional make-up will be compromised.

The chemical portion consists of electrolytes: magnesium, calcium, sodium, potassium, and a host of others. When these chemical compounds are out of balance, the body will suffer due to the lack of support that each chemical provides.

The electrical component is known as our nervous system. The sacred breath is what gives our nervous (electrical) system its power, but it is the one function we tend to understand the least. Understanding the nervous system with its many parts can be complex, but it is important to understand how it connects to our breath. Let's walk this through in simple terms.

In the earlier years of medicine, there was a symbol that was commonly used: it was an image of two snakes in opposition to one another, on a stick with a pair of eagle's wings above their heads. This symbol represented the two divisions of the nervous system, the parasympathetic and sympathetic divisions, being in balance. Ancients referred to them as the fighters. These two fighters that dwell in the nervous system are the forces that when in balance or homeostasis keep us alive. If one fighter (parasympathetic: releases too many hormones giving the human body the ability to rest and digest) is overpowered by the other (sympathetic: releases too many hormones to alert you to fight or take flight) we lose quality of life, and vice versa. There must be balance with one another for health and wellness to exist.

The sacred breath stimulates these two fighters, the parasympathetic and sympathetic, and brings them in balance, allowing the mechanical generator (the sacred breath) to charge the batteries (the heart and the kidneys), giving them the power, they need and ability to function. We all know that no matter how sophisticated batteries may be, they simply can't hold a charge forever. My body's power was almost completely depleted; I had almost completely lost 85% of my body's normal function. The doctors told me the only difference between me and a hospice patient was I wasn't lying down. My body's fighters were thrown into confusion; when I should have run from a dangerous or harmful situation, I froze, and when my body was supposed to be at rest, I was wide awake.

Let's go back to the infancy stage again to take another look at the formation of electrical power. From the birth of a child to the toddler stage, there are no concerns for the child's energy level. In fact, during these stages of development when the baby cries, they are accumulating massive charging ability and generating a reserve of electrically powered energy. By the time the child reaches the age of two, they have such an abundance of energy, just watching them will wear anyone out. Most parents can't keep up with their children's energy level without needing a nap for themselves; it's the "terrible twos" stage.

As time goes on, we are still unaware of the existence of the batteries in our body, the need to charge them, and how to charge them, and we begin to lose the reserve of our electrical power source. Without the knowledge of the body's ability to charge our electrical system through the sacred breath, we will begin to move toward our third and final component, the mechanical source, to regain strength for our waning energy. We eagerly search out methods for the strengthening our bodies (weightlifting, aerobics, running, etc.) and over time these activities become key contributors to the wear and tearing down of the mechanical components: joints, cartilage, and proper bone placement.

God never intended for mankind to depend on the physical body for a source of strength. In fact, He says those that who do are cursed. In Jeremiah 17:5, we see how the curse is unleashed. During the process of relying on oneself for strength, we are turning away from God, and whether this action is intentional or not, the results are the same. It is the turning away which indicates opposition to God. The Bible describes taking on this position as being hostile towards God. Utilizing human intellect to gain spiritual or physical strength will prove to be ineffective. This process is self-destructive and will lead to an endless and unfulfilling search for more.

Physical exercise and workout routines are commonly used in effort to regain depleting energy but will exhaust the body physically altogether. Continuing in this practice will result in the development of aching joints over time and the loss of more mechanical function as we age.

Much like exercise, loading up on other chemical compounds will bring some energy, but it will be short lived. Other energy sources may bring a quick burst of energy, but those that indulge often crash and burn later. These chemical components include caffeine and other energy drinks.

We can also look to food as an energy source, but in most cases the American diet often ultimately leads to a reduction in energy and quality of life. This occurs when we consume heavy foods, and the body lacks the electrical power to break down the food intake. For example, if you're ready for a nap just 30 minutes after you eat, it's a sign your body is lacking necessary electrical power. The food was eaten to give energy, but instead it extracts energy. This is the body's way of giving a signal that a great loss of power has taken place. This kind of indicator often gets overlooked until the body short circuits.

When Jesus was confronted by the disciples regarding his use of parables in his teaching, He explains to them that the secret of the kingdom is not given to the masses, but to those chosen. Although others may see what is happening in the natural world, they will not perceive the spiritual message and although they hear the messages, they will not understand them (Mark 4:10-12). This knowledge of the breath was a practice reserved for the ancients and taught to monks and healers and has been said to be the secret to life.

The body is intelligent and speaks to us in a variety of ways. What has been described in the above paragraph is the body's way of communicating through a variety of indicators that its systems are overloaded. The body is about to shut down into rest and digest mode in order to protect itself from short circuiting (stroking out). When too much has been put on the body, whether physically, emotionally, or mentally, the body will begin sending signals to its counterparts to shut down the least important pieces in order to continue functioning.

Think of your body as a large vessel that is traveling torrential terrains, carrying a heavy load. If at any point the safety of the vessel is being compromised by rough seas, a good captain is wise to drop some of the load in an effort to protect the crew while salvaging what he can.

As illustrated before, our body's operating system works similarly to a vehicle. The brain is the captain of our bodies, sending signals and giving commands. Putting too much food into our body at one time is one way to overload the electrical component. With a continued practice of physical, emotional, or mental overloading, many will run the risk of a short circuit (stroke). Our electrical power levels need to be higher to process increased levels of natural stressors.

Parents of most children born before the late 1960's ate a reasonably healthy diet which was generally lower in processed foods, sugars, salts, and saturated fats. This not only benefited the pregnant mom but spilled over into her baby. When the lives of most Americans changed during the baby boom generation, so did the diet. This shift in households required most people to be more creative with not only the numbers of mouths to feed, but while utilizing less time in the kitchen. This is what helped fuel the production of processed food and ignited the fast-food industry. This modern-day fast-food phenomenon has exchanged healthy mealtimes for a slow train wreck of the body's systems. The classic American diet, often filled with a touch of southern comfort, is largely responsible for the depletion of energy after most meals.

Although it's permissible to eat whatever one desires, we will reap the consequences of those choices. Man was created unaware of the existence of nakedness until the forbidden fruit was eaten. Notice what happened after they ate of the forbidden tree: they were aware of their nakedness and immediately felt shame, making coverings for themselves as they hid from God the Father (Genesis 3:7). This was the beginning of the separation between God and man, and the invitation to sickness and disease. All disease starts with improper nutrition.

In the beginning, under God's covenant, eternal provisions were made for the needs of humankind. Satan, who is our enemy (John 10:10), came to steal, kill, and destroy it. He stole our identity and caused the destruction of the covenant between us and our creator. He caused a dividing wall of hostility between the two, and without protection we have now become vulnerable to his continuous attacks. Sin killed the covenant plan for eternal life and ultimately destroyed the likeness and imagery that we once shared with God. This short act of the sinful nature opened a door to pain, sickness, and disease that was never designed for us to experience.

We have an obligation to get reacquainted with the sacred breath and to do so quickly. We must become familiar with its many functions, its power, and understand how and why we need to protect it. By releasing, restoring, and recharging the body's power and functioning capabilities inwardly, the quality of one's life is impacted overall.

We need to understand this vital force, the secrecy of the breath, and how it regenerates, resets, and restores. Satan is after it; he knows the power behind it and wants to steal it so he can maintain the power to influence what belongs to God: his children. Our flesh is the one thing

Satan has power to influence. He wants to use our flesh to steal, kill, and destroy us. Most enemies, when they can't get to you, pull your roots. They go after those that you love: your children (Revelations 12:10-12).

Because most of us lack the understanding of this sacred breath and its powers, Satan cunningly works against us, enticing many into behavior patterns that not only minimize any existing power, but eliminate any ability to recharge it. We then become more vulnerable to sickness and disease, desensitized to the destruction of our bodies caused by poor decisions, ultimately resulting in a premature death.

How do we obtain this energy source we had in our youth? We must first change the way we see it. It is the sacred breath; it is our substance for life, it is what heals all our disease, renews our strength, and is a vital force within us.

There have been many scientific studies around a variety of breathing patterns and how they can reduce anxiety, decrease depression symptoms and lower blood pressure almost instantly. This breath is a powerful tool; however, we must stop and direct our attention to it, it's effects on the body's systems and our health and wellness.

CHAPTER 3: THE SACRED BREATH IS OUR DAILY SUBSTANCE

The breath of God is our daily substance. The amount of breath we inhale daily will ultimately impact our body's systems. Remember, we are not talking about the normal daily breathing patterns. No, it's the ANCAR systematic breath patterns, specifically designed to stimulate the charging capabilities for our batteries, our power source.

This practice of reliance on a daily substance was instituted among mankind when Moses led the Israelites out of captivity. As we look back at the Israelites, we witness the constant effort God put forth to teach his chosen people the concept of total trust and dependency on him for daily substance. Exodus 16:4-5 says, "Then the Lord said to Moses, 'I will rain down bread from heaven for you. The people are to go out each day and gather enough for that day. In this way I will test them and see whether they will follow my instructions.'" As Jesus is teaching the disciples to pray, He encourages them to ask the Creator to, "Give us today our daily bread" in Matthew 6:11.

On another occasion, we see Jesus demonstrate how physical food consumption is not our only source of fuel and power. Matthew 4:1-4 says, "Then Jesus was led up by the Spirit into the wilderness to be tempted by the devil. And after fasting forty days and forty nights, he was hungry. And the tempter came and said to him, 'If you are the Son of Man, command these stones to become loaves of bread.' But he answered, 'It is written, "Man shall not live by bread alone, but by every word that comes from the mouth of God."'"

We know that the human body can go without food for roughly three weeks, yet we see Jesus push the limits of the physical by his reliance on the supernatural food.

Jesus is not simply refusing to eat bread; He is laying a very important foundation for imitation. This example serves as a lesson to many for how power can be attained through meditation. Our minds can have power over our matter (bodily forms). Through this encounter, He demonstrates exactly how we too can overcome the influence of our fleshly appetites. He himself states, "not bread alone, but every word that comes from my Father's mouth." Physical food is needed, but spiritual food is needed even more for the spiritual journey we call life. Additionally, He is demonstrating the benefits of disconnecting from the flesh and how doing so reduces much of the devil's power to influence us. Think about it for a moment: our thoughts, feelings, desires, and beliefs are part of our human makeup and are exactly what Satan influences us through. Over thinking, feeling or analyzing can cause an electrical overload of the brain and lead to a break down in the nervous system.

Remember, it's through Jesus that our connection back to God exists. God has nothing to do with sinfulness, so where does sinfulness show itself? Sin is in our fleshly nature, the nature that was shaped by the broken covenant. There are only two spirits in operation: the human spirit, where our physical flesh operates from, and the Spirit of God, which gives us the power over our flesh (Galatians 5:16-17). Live by the Spirit and you will not gratify the desires that come from the sinful nature. For the flesh desires what is contrary to the Spirit and the Spirit what is contrary to the flesh. They are in conflict with one another, so you do not do what you want.

Whichever spirit is fed and nurtured with its desired food will be the one with the most power and influence in our lives. Have you ever had a taste for a particular food that was so good that your mouth waters just thinking about it? The thought of how it was pleasing to you helped to hold the image of the dish in your mind. The flavors that swirled and danced on your palate played a role in your endless search for more of it.

Paul understood the importance of the Holy Spirit within us and it's what fueled his blunt message to the church in Galatia. It is the Spirit that gives us power over our flesh. John 3:8 says, "The wind blows wherever it pleases. You hear its sound, but you cannot tell where it comes from or where it is going. So it is with everyone born of the Spirit."

There are many hidden gems in Jesus' words that can go unnoticed. Matthew 13:10 says, "Then the disciples came and said to him, 'Why do you speak to them in parables?' He replied, 'The knowledge of the secrets of the kingdom of heaven has been given to you, but not to them.'" Matthew 13:13 says, "'This is why I speak to them in parables: though seeing, they do not see; though hearing, they do not hear or understand.'"

There are not many Naturopathic Practitioners that are aware of or practice the ANCAR 2000 series that Dr. Hapi created. He used ancient secrets and a variety of modalities to create this system. While some say, "I can do that, it's just breathing," it is more than just a normal breath pattern; it's a sacred breath practice and only a few have been given the knowledge and understanding of how to use it properly.

Mark 1:35 says, "Very early in the morning, while it was still dark, Jesus got up, left the house and went off to a solitary place, where he prayed." In this passage we witness Jesus seeking out God for his daily substance. This breath system also serves as a daily practice for building and maintaining the body's systems and overall function.

In John 4:13-14, while Jesus was waiting for the disciples to return from purchasing food, he talked with a Samaritan woman and offered her a new and living way to quench the thirst of her flesh. This woman not only recounted her previous failed attempts at satisfying her thirst but recognized that her flesh would never be fully satisfied. Something shifted, and she knew that only through the true Messiah would true satisfaction ever be possible.

Jesus spent a great length of time teaching the disciples how to move away from the flesh for substance and instead cling to the Spirit. After the disciples returned with the food they had purchased, they noticed Jesus was not partaking in the food and they encouraged him to eat. "Meanwhile his disciples urged him, 'Rabbi, eat something'. But he said to them, 'I have food to eat that you know nothing about.' Then his disciples said to each other, 'Could someone have brought him food?'" (John 4:31-34). Jesus used this as another opportunity to teach them, but again they missed out on the lesson. Jesus was referring to his nourishment coming from our heavenly Father in a supernatural form (meditating on God's Word).

As we continue our spiritual journey, we must also recognize the lessons we've missed. Jesus is trying to help us to move away from the one thing Satan has his greatest influence over: our flesh. Prayer was not merely an assignment Jesus checked off his daily spiritual acts list, but it is an intentional act and acknowledgment of His need for God's provision. His actions demonstrate total trust and dependency on God the Father to give Him what was needed to carry out His will. We must follow this practice. Jesus began and ended his day with prayer and meditation on God's Word (Luke 21:37).

The ANCAR 2000 series is not simply a meditation but is a spiritual practice and form of alternative medicine that aims to provide physical relaxation and mental clarity. Meditation is usually practiced in a seated position with eyes closed and with the focus on the pineal gland. This area is located deep in the center of the brain. While your eyes are closed you can focus your sight between your two eyes, commonly referred to as the third eye.

The pineal gland has a structure much like an eye, and although it does not share any of the eye's normal functions, it has a light receptor that relates to our senses. When our focus is completely locked in, we stimulate the pineal gland which releases hormones. One hormone is called melatonin, which causes the body to relax.

In this relaxed state, mediation allows the mind, when focused, to bring in and hold to positive affirmations about God, his Word, or other good thoughts, and allows the mind, body, and spirit to connect to that held belief.

During the inhalation process, we are breathing in oxygen which passes through the alveoli, the part of the respiratory system where oxygen and carbon dioxide molecules are exchanged going to and from the bloodstream.

While exhaling, one can release any fears, anxieties, or negative thoughts. The process of exhalation is of great importance, as it releases toxins from the body. 1 Peter 5:6-7 says, "Cast all your anxiety on him because he cares for you." "Cast" means to throw, and prayer and meditation is reserved for the releasing or laying of our burdens at the feet of the Lord (Matthew 11:28-30).

There are many health benefits to meditation and God commands us to meditate on his Word. When we connect with our breath, we are connecting to the Spirit of God. As we focus our thoughts on his Word, it becomes what nourishes us and takes away our thirst for fleshy forms of nourishment. It does not mean we'll never eat physical food again; it simply means that our greatest consumption of any substance will be from the hand of God. Like Proverbs 2:10 says, "Wisdom will enter your heart and knowledge will be pleasant to your soul."

As we learned from Jesus, the devil can't offer God's elect anything that will be enough to fill us. When we allow our substance to come from God, we won't hunger for what the devil is offering, because we know God gives us power, energy, and everything we need.

CHAPTER 4: THE SACRED BREATH IS OUR COUNSELOR

The sacred breath is our counselor. Many people seek therapy or a counselor as an acknowledgement or acceptance that their life, or a particular situation, has become unmanageable on their own.

The practice of this breath work can bring one experiencing very high-level stressful situations, or those in crisis, to a calm state. It takes us into a state of consciousness where we can connect to the spiritual realm inside ourselves which we were created from.

When the direct connection to God was broken, we became vulnerable to Satan's influence and attacks through our flesh including our emotions, feelings, and thoughts. We know that Jesus is the only way back to the Father. It is summarized in this statement: "For the Son of Man came to seek and save what was lost" (Luke 19:10). What was lost? Our connection to our spiritual Father; our identity and original versions of ourselves as co-creators with the creator who formed us.

Let's look back at Jesus' life after his baptism. Mathew 4:16 says, "As soon as Jesus was baptized, he went up out of the water. At that moment heaven was opened, and he saw the Spirit of God descending like a dove and lightening on him. And a voice from heaven said, 'This is my son, whom I love; with him I am well pleased.'"

Let us to focus our attention on the moment that Jesus exits the watery grave in baptism. It was then, during that rebirthing process, that heaven was opened, and the power of the sacredness came and rested upon him. After this takes place, we witness his incredible spiritual strengthening and resistance to the flesh. We see this same power displayed on the day of Pentecost. When the day of Pentecost came, the disciples were all together in one place. Suddenly a sound like the blowing of a violent wind came from heaven and filled the whole house where they were sitting. They saw what seemed to be tongues of fire that separated and came to rest on each of them. All were filled with the Holy Spirit and began to speak in other tongues as the Spirit enabled them to (Acts 2:2-4). Could this re-birthing be a restoration of the lost connection with the Holy Spirit through the sacred breath? Perhaps it is.

Notice the descriptive words used to describe this sacred breath: "like a dove," which depicts gentleness, and "lighting" which depicts its' incredible power. We can witness this same power of the Spirit's consultation unfold again and again as Jesus walked among the people.

In Matthew 4:3 and 4:5, we see the power to resist the desires of the flesh. Jesus knew if he sought after the things of his flesh, he would disqualify himself as Savior, and those things would ultimately become objects of worship. He responds to the devil with the truth. "For it is written: 'worship the Lord your God and serve him only.'"

In Matthew 4:17, we see the power of knowledge and authority as Jesus begins to preach on repentance.

In Matthew 4:18, we see the power of influence as he calls Simon and his brother Andrew to follow him into his ministry.

In Matthew 4:23-24, we see the power of compassion as he teaches the people and begins healing their diseases.

In Matthew 5-7, we see the power of wisdom and discernment in His teaching. Although His message was consistent, with one standard for all who followed him, Jesus uses a variety of delivery methods that spoke to each individual person.

In Matthew 8:1-4, we see the power to heal and make new as Jesus heals a man from leprosy, giving him new flesh from a disease that impacted the body from the inside out.

In Matthew 8:28-34, we see the power to grant mercy at the request of demons that worked against Him as He cast them out of two men.

In Matthew 9:27-30, we see the power to show mercy as He heals the blind and mute.

In Matthew 10:1, we see the power of discernment to give authority when Jesus pulls the disciples together after training to empower them to do the work of God.

In Matthew 11:28-30, we see the power to be humble and come to God when we are weary and burdened.

In Matthew 12:22-32, we see the power to stand alone while Jesus faces off with the Pharisees regarding His ability to cast out demons.

In Matthew 13:53-58, we see the power of God to handle those that come against or try to discredit you.

In Matthew 14:16-20, we see the power of looking to God for provision, while resisting the urge to rely on self.

In Matthew 15:21-28, we see the power of discernment demonstrated through an act of kindness as Jesus grants favor to a people not belonging to God.

In Matthew 16:21-23, we see the power of vulnerability demonstrated through His sharing the painful experiences to come.

In Matthew 17:25-27, we see the power of humility as Jesus does not use equality with God as leverage to avoid the laws of the land.

In Matthew 18:21-35, we see the power to forgive at the heart level through the foundational teachings of Jesus.

In Matthew 19:16-30, we see the power of eternal perspective as Jesus speaks with the rich man on how to possess eternal life.

In Matthew 20:20-23, we see the power of gentleness as Jesus speaks with the mother of Zebedee's sons regarding her request for her sons to sit at the right and left side of him in the kingdom.

In Matthew 21:23-27, we see the power of shrewdness while Jesus' authority is questioned by the Pharisees.

In Matthew 22:15-22, we see the power of patience as the Pharisees try to trap Jesus.

In Matthew 23:1-39, we see the power of integrity as Jesus addresses the religious leaders for preaching, teaching, and holding the people of God accountable to the law, while excluding themselves.

In Matthew 24:1-51, we see the power of truth as Jesus teaches the disciples how to stay free from lies that are set as traps, and how determine the signs of his return.

In Matthew 25, we see the power of stewardship as Jesus teaches the disciples that they have an obligation to fulfill all the righteous requirements He set in place and a responsibility to be the eyes, hands, and feet of God in His absence.

In Matthew 26:17-28, we see the power to balance emotions as Jesus is preparing to die for all, even the one who will betray Him.

In Matthew 26:31, we see the power to deal with abandonment, as Jesus is aware of them all falling away.

In Matthew 25:33, we see the power to deal with emotional trauma as Jesus prepares for His impending crucifixion.

In John 14:16, Jesus tells the disciples, "I will ask the Father, and he will give you another Counselor to be with you forever, the Spirit of truth." At this moment the day of Pentecost had not yet come, but Jesus was preparing them for the arrival. He explains how the Counselor will remind them of all that He had taught them.

Jesus tells them that they know the way to the place he is preparing. They have the secrets to an eternal connection with God the Father, the Son, and the Holy Spirit (John 14:1-4).

John 14:12-14 says, "'I tell you the truth, anyone who has faith in me will do what I have been doing. He will do even greater things than these, because I'm going to the Father. And I will do whatever you ask in my name, so that the son may bring glory to the Father. You may ask me for anything in my name, and I will do it.'"

Most counselors in the world of therapy mirror back to us the true image of ourselves, removing any smoke-filled perceptions, lies, or blind spots. Consider the possibility of the Creator granting those that take time to practice this system an open pathway to seeing, feeling, and experiencing Him in new ways. This experience has been transformative, powerful, and comforting (2 Corinthians 1:1-7).

CHAPTER 5: THE SACRED BREATH IS OUR VITAL FORCE

The sacred breath is a vital force. Vital implies that it is necessary, yet we don't know enough about it and give so little attention to protecting it. It's amazing to see how the body can go roughly three days without water and three weeks without food yet can go no more than three minutes without breath before parts of the brain die off.

When parts of the brain begin to die as a result of lack of oxygen, very important brain signals stop functioning as well. This demonstrates the significance of the sacred breath.

We know that breath provides life, but there are other important functions of the breath. Our breath is one of our primary forms of communicating with God and others. We use our body, sign language, thoughts, attitudes, and actions to communicate. With our breath, we speak, pray, sing, and praise God. Our breath is what gives us our power to reflect the image of God. This vital force is not only the transportation of the oxygen that our body runs on; it is our power source. This power source is how our body's internal alternator and batteries are charged.

No human can recall what it was like to take their very first breath. I wonder what would happen if we all had the opportunity to go back to our birthing process with the knowledge we gained from this book. Would it change how we use this powerful gift? I'd like to think that it would.

Understanding the unleashing power this vital force plays in our lives is critical. I hope this book gives you the inspiration needed to foster a new appreciation for the sacred breath. I pray that it challenges you to breathe deeper with each passing moment. Most of all, I hope it changes the way you see this amazing gift and utilize it for its intended purpose.

TESTIMONIES

Author's note: Another modality that is equally important to the health and wellness process is grounding or earthing. I was introduced to this practice by my neighbor, Jason. I invited Jason, alongside a few others, to share their story.

Jason Irvin
In 2017, I was sick, lost, and desperately searching for answers. Ever since I was a kid, my eating habits were horrendous. I ate what I wanted, when I wanted, and how much I wanted. Everything finally caught up to me. One day, while I was making a routine trip to the bathroom, I noticed something that I had never seen before. I was shocked at the presence of blood flowing through my urine and into the toilet.

At first, I didn't pay it much mind. I figured it would be a one-off occasion. "This too shall pass," I thought to myself. But I was in for a journey that I never expected to experience.

The presence of blood continued to recur. Eventually, the blood further developed into major discomfort near my pelvic area and lower abdomen. It felt like a baseball was sitting inside of me and I could feel the pain traveling down my left leg.

Confused and scared, I scheduled the first of many doctors' visits. I made more trips to the doctor's office and emergency room than I can remember. At first, my primary doctor was not exactly sure what we were dealing with, but she knew it related to the urinary system. After further consultations, I was prescribed medication for the pain. When it proved effective for only a period, my doctor advised me to see a urologist.

After an exam, the urologist advised that I undergo a cystoscopy in order to take a microscopic look at the prostate. The results determined I was experiencing an enlarged prostate. The doctors who performed the procedure informed me that the cause of an enlarged prostate is the overconsumption of acidic foods, such as coffee, alcohol, many pizza sauces, fried foods, processed foods, fast foods, and the like. Outside of the coffee, they accurately described my lifestyle. Never before that point in my life did I fathom that what we eat and drink could impact our bodies internally in the way it was impacting me.

I thought I was healthy. I thought I was in shape. I had visibly defined abs. I was a personal trainer. I worked out for a living. I did cardio consistently. I should be healthy, right? I was sadly mistaken. I was prescribed more medication, but the flare ups continued. After yet another visit and a stronger prescription, it finally dawned on me what the doctors had told me: it's all in what we eat and drink.

From that day forward, I vowed to never take the medication again. I went home and embarked on a journey of discovering natural ways to heal the body. Along with changing the way I ate; I learned about a phenomenon called grounding. I was intrigued. From my research, I learned that "grounding" or "earthing" is the process of placing our bare feet, hands, or any other exposed part of our bodies in direct contact with the earth (soil, grass, sand, trees, etc.) in order to regulate an overly stressed nervous system. When inflammation in our bodies is reduced, we feel better. I immediately began to try it out for myself. Instantly, I felt relief in my body that I had never felt before. I felt calm. I felt peace. I felt understanding. I felt closer to God. I began telling everyone about it. I promoted it on social media. Many people thought I was crazy. Some tried it, while others passed. By the grace of God, I was fortunate enough to connect with other people who were on the same journey, so I kept at it.

Grounding sparked fresh energy back into my life. I stayed consistent with it. Then one day, as I stood outside in the grass with my shoes and socks off, feet one with the ground, my neighbor, D'Lana, approached me. By the look on her face, I could tell she was intrigued, yet skeptical. I told her what I was doing and how it was helping my body to heal from years of trauma. We held a conversation that ended with D'Lana mentioning to me that she would consider giving grounding a try the next morning.

As I rose out of bed, I did what I always did: I began my day by looking out the window to catch a glimpse of nature and all its beauty. I was amazed by what I saw. D'Lana kept to her word: she was outside, in her backyard near the fire pit, praising God, with her bare feet connected to the earth. A smile of gratitude came across my face. From that day forward, D'Lana was hooked. I saw her outside grounding just about every day. She later inquired about how to continue her practice once winter set in. I pointed her towards official websites that provided grounding materials such as mats, pillows, sheets, etc.

Why grounding, you might ask? When we look around the world into our overcrowded cities, you'll notice that we have lost our connection with nature. The platforms claiming to connect us are actually what disconnect us from nature and one another. By nature, our bodies are electrical and so is the earth, filled with deep reservoirs of free electrons. When we are connected with it, the earth helps charge the human body to help us function at our best.

With the advancement of technology in our modern world, we are bombarded with harmful EMFs (Electro Magnetic Frequencies). Wi-Fi, cell phone towers, skyscrapers, and modes of transportation, amongst other systems, all contribute to the environmental pollution that causes harm to our internal cells and their functioning capabilities. These EMFs can slow transmission and/or disrupt normal brain wave activity. By reducing usage of these devices and connecting back to the earth, we can begin to regain our waning power.

Along with grounding I have recently added breath work to my daily routine. Not long ago, D'Lana introduced me to the ANCAR 2000 breathing system. During my first session, near the end of the practice, I felt my inhalation capacity increase. After the first week, I saw a drastic change in my mental clarity and workout performance.

Today, as a Certified Personal Trainer and Health and Wellness Advocate, I have partnered with D'Lana and a host of other health practitioners dedicated to supporting the mind, body, and spirit through natural health solutions. If you or someone you know can benefit from these services, please feel free to reach out to me.

Instagram: jayswervinfitness
TikTok: jayswervinfitnes
YouTube: JaySwervinFitness

Dr. Patricia Jones Blessman
Being introduced to this breath work by D'Lana has been an incredible gift. Like many others, I used to take breathing for granted. We never really think about it.

Initially, I wasn't all that enthusiastic about beginning an intentional or intensified breath practice like this. However, I was thoroughly surprised at the results the ANCAR 2000 breathing system had on my body's overall physicality. This practice has made a significant change in the way I see and connect with the life force around me.

You might ask how often someone should do this breath work to enjoy these same benefits. My answer is, do it only on the days you want to feel good!

Breathing is more than something that just happens. It's an intentional act of taking in life-giving air that enriches each cell in our body for its highest functioning capability. Completing this practice daily has not only been instrumental in my body's operating systems but has also improved the quality of the life I live. As a health advocate, I now get to share that with others.

Alex Blunt

In 2017 I was invited to an ANCAR 2000 demonstration by D'Lana. I heard about it on several occasions, but as a Certified Personal Trainer and an NCAA and IHSA Coach, I was not impressed with what was said. I thought it was just a simple breathing practice and didn't think it would prove to be as effective as stated.

Reluctantly, I went to the event and at first glance, everything seemed as I thought it would be. Then it happened: Dr. Hapi called me up to be used as an example of how the practice worked. At first, I was extremely skeptical about doing the breath work. I laid on the table and we began the demonstration. He had me do 30 breath repetitions with a very specific speed and I struggled through. That's right—me, the Certified Personal Trainer and coach, struggled to do just 30 breaths. After I completed the practice, he called an 80-year-old client of his and had her lie on the table. She completed 1800 breaths at a much faster speed, and I was shocked. Not only did she do it without a struggle; she didn't even break a sweat. I was so humbled. I asked the doctor for a hug and said, "I'm a believer in this practice."

I started the practice shortly after and saw changes in my stamina and mental clarity. Even today, it continues to improve. I have since incorporated utilizing the breath as my primary source of strength rather than the muscles that come with natural mechanical movement. I have also incorporated the ANCAR 2000 breathing system in all fitness routines and coaching strategies. I have seen an increase in my strength training significantly. In one month, my dead lift PR increased over 100lbs. My core is overall stronger. It naturally suppresses my appetite and reduces my craving for snacks. When working with my younger athletes using this breathing system, I've seen an improvement in their focus and discipline. They are better able to self-regulate during the high stress periods in the games.

This breath work is a cutting-edge technique and my personal secret weapon that sets my players apart from all the others. With increased speed and quick strategic thinking, my players have consistent stamina throughout the game. I'm so very thankful for the introduction to this practice; it has been life changing.

If you or someone you know could benefit from a credible fitness, life, or basketball coaching experience, reach out to me.

Instagram: @theycallmecoach1200 @motion_elite
Webpage: Motionelitebasketball.com

About the Author

In December 2019, she retired from Local-Motions and shortly after, started Unshackled Ministries. Her vision was to provide unconventional support for the mind, body, and spirit through natural health solutions. As a Board-Certified Health Practitioner, (American Association of Drugless Practitioners) (Trinity School of Natural Health), and Mental Health Practitioner (Light University and American Association for Christian Counselors), she has been committed to this especially important body of work.

If you have enjoyed The Sacred Breath, check out these writings.

Revision Coming Soon

UNSHACKLED

Unveiling many truths after the shackles come off reveals the true level of freedom. Long after shackles are removed, some can remain bound to behavior patterns developed because of traumatic experiences. This can leave one unable to discover, embrace, or explore the freedom Christ offers those who dare follow him.

Coming Soon

BROKEN MIRRORS

Don't blame the mirror, change the image!

We all have a story to tell of how our life's experiences have fashioned us into who we are today. Our lives are like mirrors, reflecting images, while telling the stories of our pain, trauma, and fears. A mirror can't take the blame for the reflection of the image or the story it tells. It only provides a solid testimony and supports the evidence of what we've ignored, avoided, or tried to hide.

THE DOSE

Every human being was created by God and born to be part of a royal priesthood. The fabrics of our beings were carefully woven together through our life's experiences while we grew and developed. *The Dose* is filled with daily spiritual perspectives that will help you recapture the image you were created in.

www.ingramcontent.com/pod-product-compliance
Lightning Source LLC
Chambersburg PA
CBHW042333150426
43194CB00001B/48